Welcome To

I SPY SOMETHING WITH MY LITTLE EYE

This Book Belongs To

....
....
....

I SPY with my little eye something beginning with

It's an

Avocado

I SPY with my little eye something beginning with

It's a

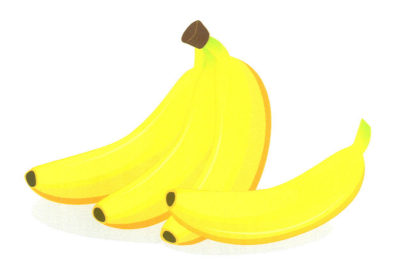

Banana

I SPY with my little eye something beginning with

It's a

Candy

I SPY with my little eye something beginning with

It's a

Demon

I spy with my little eye something beginning with

It's an

Elf

I spy with my little eye something beginning with

It's a

Frankenstein

I SPY with my little eye something beginning with

It's a

Grape

I SPY with my little eye something beginning with

It's a

Hat

I SPY with my little eye something beginning with I

It's an

Imp

I SPY with my little eye something beginning with

It's a

Joker

I spy with my little eye something beginning with

It's a

Kiwi

I SPY with my little eye something beginning with

It's a

Lemon

I SPY with my little eye something beginning with

It's a

Mango

I SPY with my little eye something beginning with

It's a

Nectarine

I SPY with my little eye something beginning with

It's an

Orange

I SPY with my little eye something beginning with

It's a

Pumpkin

I SPY with my little eye something beginning with

It's a

Queen

I spy with my little eye something beginning with

It's a

Raven

I SPY with my little eye something beginning with

It's The End

Printed in the USA
CPSIA information can be obtained
at www.ICGtesting.com
LVHW070744031124
795554LV00030B/178